TO:_____

_____

FROM:_____

_____

DATE:_____

_____

Published by Christian Art Publishers
PO Box 1599, Vereeniging, 1930, RSA

© 2015
First edition 2015

Cover designed by Christian Art Publishers

Images used under license from Shutterstock.com

Printed in China

ISBN 978-1-4321-1489-3

16   17   18   19   20   21   22   23   24   25   –   21   20   19   18   17   16   15   14   13   12

BE STILL

and know that I am God.

COLORING BOOK

Coloring therapy with Scripture verses from Psalms

CHRISTIAN ART PUBLISHERS

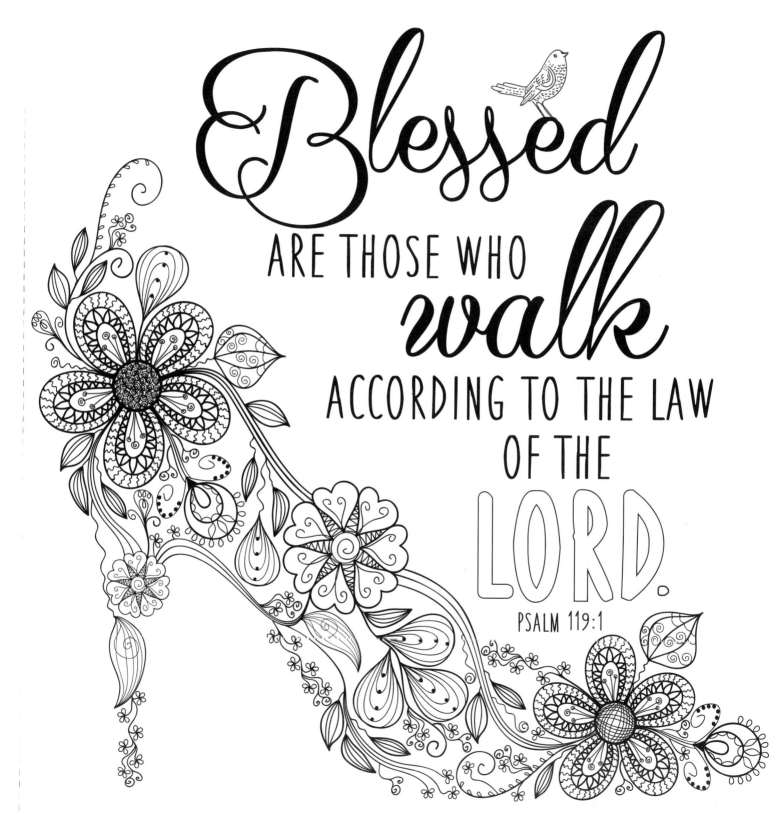

Blessed
ARE THOSE WHO
walk
ACCORDING TO THE LAW
OF THE
LORD.
PSALM 119:1

THE WORD OF THE LORD IS RIGHT & TRUE; HE IS FAITHFUL IN ALL HE DOES.
PSALM 33:4

Praise the Lord from the EARTH, you creatures of the OCEAN depths.

Psalm 148:7

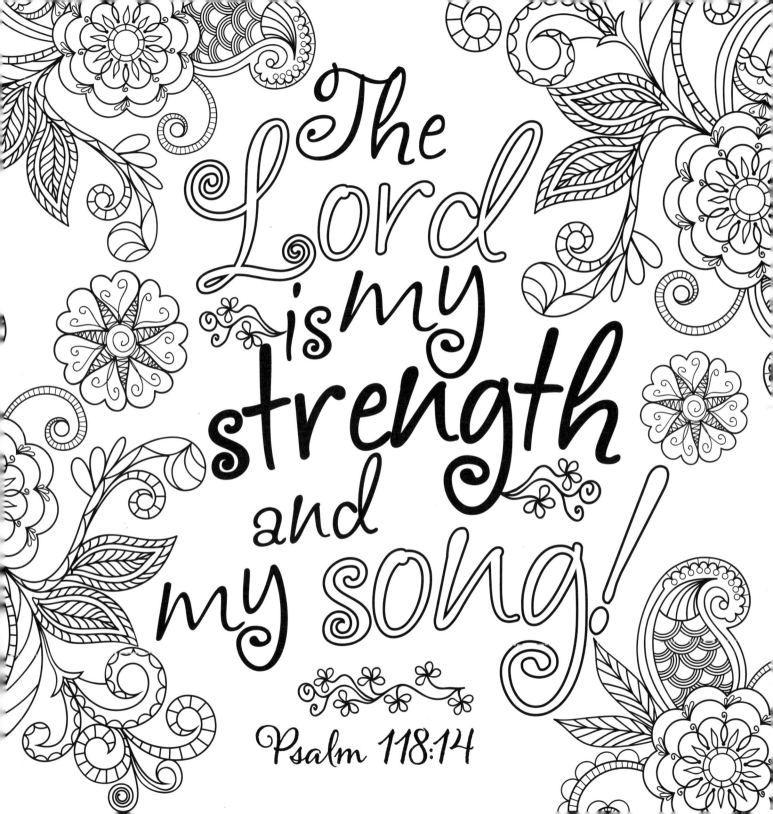

LET THE
HEARTS
OF THOSE WHO
SEEK
THE LORD
REJOICE
PSALM 105:3

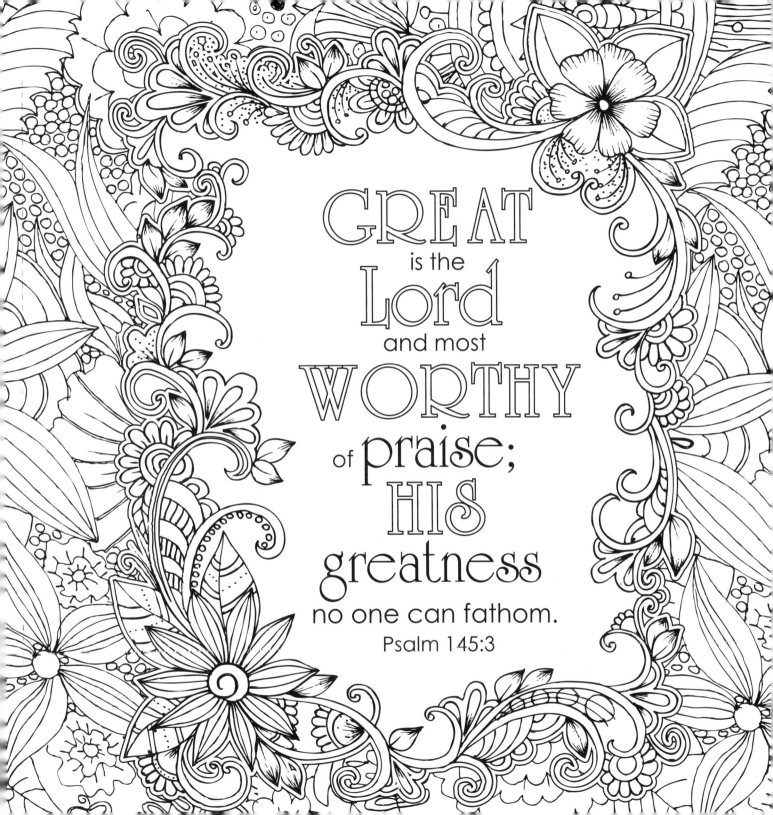

GREAT
is the
Lord
and most
WORTHY
of praise;
HIS
greatness
no one can fathom.
Psalm 145:3

In Him our hearts rejoice, for we trust in His holy name. Psalm 33:21

Sing to the LORD a new song, for He has done marvelous things.

Psalm 98:1

DO GOOD.
SEARCH
FOR
peace
AND
work
TO MAINTAIN IT.

PSALM 34:14

HE fills MY life WITH good THINGS.

PSALM 103:5

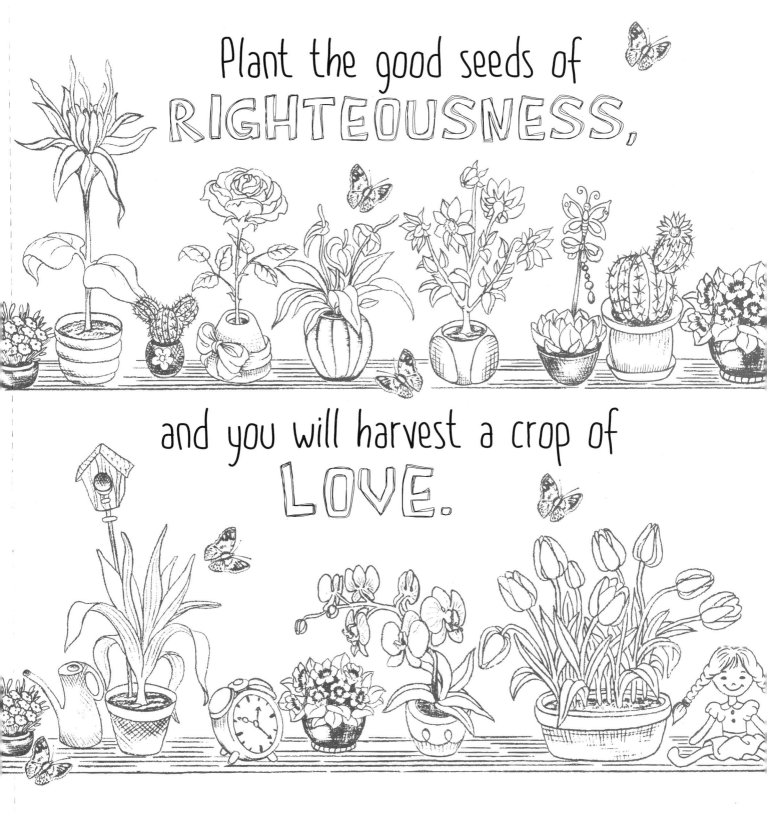

LORD, You alone ARE MY inheritance, MY CUP OF blessing. You GUARD ALL that is mine.

PSALM 16:5

ALL THE
EARTH
BOWS DOWN TO
YOU, O GOD;
THEY
SING
THE
PRAISES OF YOUR
NAME

PSALM 66:4

GOD IS THE KING OF ALL THE EARTH;

SING TO HIM A PSALM OF PRAISE.

Psalm 47:7

The
whole earth
is filled with
awe at Your
wonders.
Psalm 65:8

As high as the heavens are above the earth, so great is His love for those who fear Him. Psalm 103:11

Give thanks to the Lord of lords
endures forever.
who by His understanding made the heavens, who
to govern the day, the moon and stars to govern the night.
Lord, for He is good. His love endures forever.
to govern the night. Psalm 136:1-9

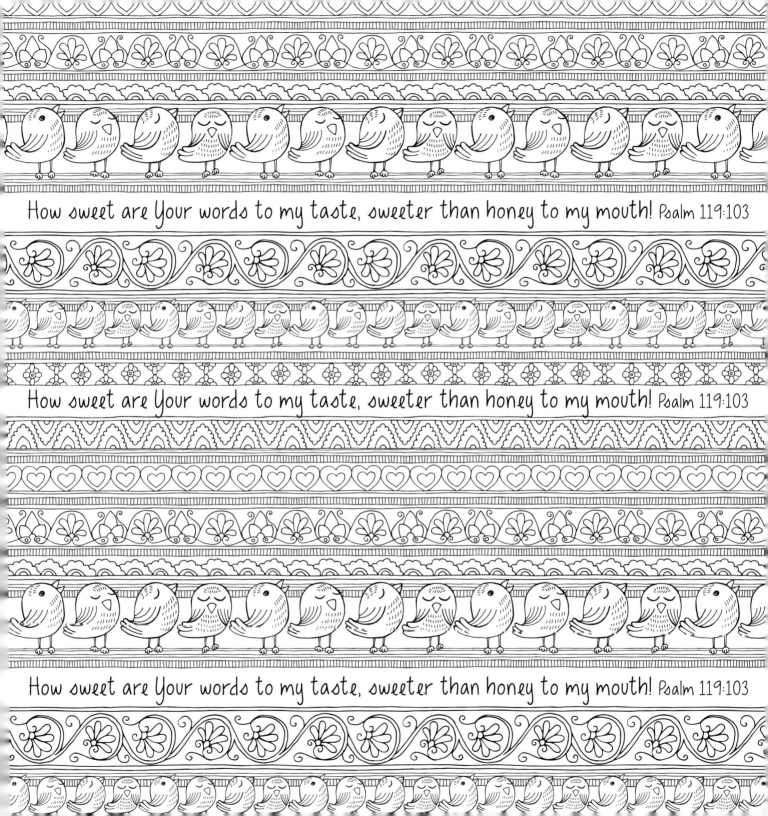

How sweet are Your words to my taste, sweeter than honey to my mouth! Psalm 119:103

How sweet are Your words to my taste, sweeter than honey to my mouth! Psalm 119:103

How sweet are Your words to my taste, sweeter than honey to my mouth! Psalm 119:103

Cards TO COLOR, CUT & FOLD

Rejoice in the Lord always! Philippians 4:4

OWL ALWAYS LOVE YOU!

I always thank my God for you. 1 Corinthians 1:4

FOLDING LINE

FOLDING LINE

PLACE IN MY HEART. YOU HAVE A SPECIAL

PHILIPPIANS 1:7

LOVE

May the Lord *bless you & keep you.*

Numbers 6:24

A sweet friendship *refreshes* the soul.

PROVERBS 27:9